NOTES TO SELF

30 Days of Notes and Affirmations to Help Promote Personal Growth

Brian P.

Notes To Self:
30 Days of Notes and Affirmations to Help Promote Personal Growth
© 2023 Brian P

Destination Elevation Publishing
https://destinationelevationpublishing.com

All rights reserved.

In memory of my parents, may this book be a tribute to your never-ending belief in me with unceasing love.

Acknowledgements

First and foremost, I give all honor and praises to God, the head of my entire life for His continuous grace and mercy. I also thank Him for the precious memories and time granted with my mother and father on this side. Their teachings, love, and guidance live on forever.

To my wife Pamela, you are incredible to say the least. My son LB, my daughter-in love Toya and their children, Sariah, Syncere, Brylin (Tootie), and Aries. My son Chris, my daughter in love, Jai, and Cai. You all are my why as I attempt to build an empire to leave a legacy. To my Myah who came and changed my entire life, making me better and younger, please stay 11 forever.

To my sisters Tina, Marshelle, Carolyn, Star, and my brother Charles, I thank God for you all and love you to the end of life and back.

Disclaimer: Contents in the book are for informational purposes only. I encourage you to seek professional advice in any areas needed.

TABLE OF CONTENTS

Prologue ix

Foreword xi

The Subconscious Mind xvii

Reprogram The Subconscious Mind for Success xxi

Objective 1

Notes to Self
- *Let It All Go* 2
- *Change and Growth* 6
- *Welcoming Challenges* 10
- *Raising Standards* 14
- *Mind Over Matter* 18
- *True Wealth* 22
- *The Same Place* 26
- *Stepping Out of The Box* 30
- *Attitude* 34
- *Comfort Zone* 38
- *Surrounded by Success* 42
- *Communicating* 46
- *Assets and Liabilities* 50
- *Control* 54
- *It's Necessary* 58
- *Production & Consumption* 62
- *Priorities* 66
- *Self-Contained* 70
- *A Gift* 74
- *Setting Standards* 78
- *My Purpose* 82

Liberation 86

Success 90

Perceptions 94

Fell and Fail 98

Pain 102

The Picture 106

Completion 110

Competing 114

Accountability 118

Meet The Author 124

Prologue

Notes to Self is an anthology of empowerment quotations and affirmations. Many are personally designed to project and stimulate the mind, maneuvering the self-driven individual into a different way of thinking. This book can also be considered an aid to remind some, and instruct others, to never stop reaching for personal goals. I hungered for this type of insight at a younger age. However, later I realized that it would have been more than I could comprehend at that time.

I have made many mistakes along with bad decisions that cost me and some people around me. During my younger years, I was never one to make a mistake and learn from it right away. When you understand what's right and you still keep going left, you realize it's no longer a mistake, it's poor decision-making. This is the time when I was changing, but not growing.

This book was inspired by self-evaluation, my own successes, and many not so successful attempts at growth and expansion over a period of time. Or, as I like to call it, my, "blood, sweat, and years." It took a period of several years to complete many of the goals I'd positioned myself for. Had I known then, what I know now, perhaps I would have arrived at my destination in a fraction of that time.

My journey to success in my own right reminds me of a story I was told about a man and his son as they were walking along a dirt road. The son wanted to impress his father and told his dad that he could move a rock alongside the road that was almost taller and much heavier than he. The father, knowing his son was too small, calmly replied, "I'm sure you can son, but only if you use all of your strength." The energized son made several unsuccessful attempts to move the rock, but it was too weighty and would not budge.

In total disappointment, the son stated, "I used every bit of my strength Dad, but I couldn't move the rock." The dad replied, "Wrong son, you didn't ask me to help." The moral to this story is I had to recognize all my strength and how to utilize it at the moment, I received the results that I had sought noticing the power of a subconscious mind in a continuous alliance with conscious efforts.

Foreword

After serving my debt to society of completing 12 years in prison, which included two years of solitary confinement, I took my first breaths of freedom. I was able to fill my lungs with air of the world that I had almost forgotten existed. With each step taken away from my past life, I could feel the weight of my mistakes slowly releasing its hold on my soul.

I was determined to change my mindset from the chains of a prisoner to the wings of a free and happy person. After surrounding myself with positive influences, I sought out books and knowledgeable individuals who could help shape my thoughts and expand my horizons.

Changing my mindset yielded remarkable results and afforded me the opportunity to rebuild my life and share my story with others. Genuine change is not solely about moving past one's mistakes: it's about using those mistakes as steppingstones to a brighter future. My release from prison not only freed me from physical confinement, but also unlocked the power within me to change my entire thought process.

Once considered a menace to society, I have since become an advocate for criminal justice reform using my own story to raise awareness and push for positive change. By choosing to embrace a mindset shift, positive change and a newfound life purpose, I've transformed my life and become an agent for change for myself and those around me. My journey to becoming mentally and emotionally focused regarding my past was a hard one, which pushed me to my limits at times. I've had countless hours of self-awareness and self-reflection moments that helped me to get acquainted with a newer and better version of myself.

Twelve years in prison was not easy, however, it was necessary to go through what I did to get to where I am. It's been proven that even the darkest chapters of one's life can be rewritten with the power of a changed mindset so if you ever need a witness, here I am.

After five years, I am now founder of Peace4Poverty, a nonprofit organization focusing on educating those in underserved communities. We do this by career training in various business fields that lead to successful entrepreneurship.

If you're reading this short Foreword, then you have made the right decision in purchasing this book humbly written by my friend Brian. Please utilize his version of mental notes and affirmations then produce your own within spaces provided to become more aware and self-reflect.

Joshua Proby
Founder, Peace4Poverty
Author, 30 Day Journey From Prison to Spiritual Peace
International Speaker
Activist

"Our subconscious minds have no sense of humor, play no jokes, and cannot tell the difference between reality *and* imagined thought or image. What we continually think about even and eventually will manifest in our lives."
- Robert Collier

"We have the hidden potential to affirm our way in the direction of an abundance of progress, *growth*, and increase. By networking with like-minded individuals and applying affirmations you'll soon discover yourself on a voyage of purpose and transformation. The application of knowledge is power."

-Brian P.

The Subconscious Mind

Although many of us understand we have an incredible power source called the subconscious mind, there are few of us who know much more about it than that. Let alone, the influential force it can have on our overall pursuit for success and personal growth. This is unfortunate because our subconscious mind can be the deciding aspect of whether we're able to accomplish certain goals or tasks. Some may ask what exactly is the subconscious mind and how does it function? Well, I'm glad you asked.

The answer is simple and not as complex as many may assume. Your subconscious mind is the powerhouse of who you really are or can be. Think of your mind as a computer and how much information is received and processed daily. During extensive research, I found it's believed that our minds can produce an estimated 10 quadrillion calculations per second without us even knowing it, just to paint a picture. There are many places to store information such as files, documents, and pictures on your computer and numerous ways to increase your storage capacity when needed.

Imagine a top grade and highly sophisticated supercomputer with tons of storage capacity. However, the human mind is by far more advanced, and its storage capacity is without comparison. The information that we accumulate remains wherever we store it for later use. Also, think of it as the mental storage area for everything that's not in your conscious mind.

I can go all day giving countless examples, but the human mind is directly held accountable for the triggering of certain emotions and feelings when we're suddenly faced with arriving at the threshold of new and intimidating situations.

All our habits of thinking and acting are stored in our subconscious mind, and because of this it has memorized all our boundaries of comfort and effortlessly keeps us within them. It keeps us within them by causing us to feel emotionally useless whenever we attempt to try something new.

Instead of breaking this cycle, most choose to remain in a zone of comfort because it's much safer there.

Sadly, after years of not understanding how to fracture this paradigm, it has caused countless individuals to repeatedly abandon opportunity when presented with it. Have you ever wondered why some people are wealthier, more successful, and even at times appear more intelligent? It's not because they've found the secret to success and riches.

The answer is they know the real meaning of the old saying of, "working smarter versus working harder." Simply put, some have tapped into the hidden treasure and potential of their subconscious mind. In doing so, utilizing certain measures along with their continuous efforts has caused many to prosper. Adapting this exact mindset and mentality, can create even more opportunity for us and our families.

A recent study was conducted of one hundred men and women who were interviewed and questioned about the subconscious mind. Surprisingly, over half were aware of their subconscious mind and its capability. However, when asked what, if anything, prevented them from achieving their goals, over half of them gave an answer in one word, fear. It's no surprise that fear of the unknown and the fear of success are common issues among millions and that's the bad news.

The good news is that they can be corrected during the reprogramming of the subconscious mind, which is often compared to self-hypnosis, but please don't be terrified by my choice of words. Our subconscious runs our lives and if we grant permission, it will also destroy our lives. Therefore, it is most beneficial that we program it to function in the manner we want it to. Once reprogrammed, then we can have more of the things we want in our existence and live to our full potential, which should be the ultimate objective.

Reprogram the Subconscious Mind for Success

Unbeknownst to many of us, the subconscious mind contains a powerful and limitless supply of untapped potential, giving us the capability to heal ourselves. Reprogramming our minds offers unlimited benefits such as making our personal and professional lives much less stressful, always giving clarity of thought, super easy access to life resolutions, and understanding the root of our phobias. My advice is to reprogram the intelligence with scientifically intended training and then track its progress.

Affirm- to state or assert positively; maintain as true.

Affirmation is the key ingredient needed for apparent abundance. It works to transform our subconscious intellect by using optimistic, personal, and present tense statements to dominate our negative intelligence and judgment. Daily affirmations work best as they should be kept upbeat primarily focusing on what we want to happen soon versus what we want to stop happening.

To penetrate our subconscious, there should be no limit to our affirmations and should be included in every activity of the day. Distractions must be kept to a minimum. Keep negative elements and thinking absent as you attempt to embed affirmations into your subconscious. Entertaining corrupt thoughts will hinder progress defeating the total purpose.

Visualize- to recall or reform mental images or pictures.

The act of creating detailed mental images that illustrate a preferred outcome, so you may envision yourself in a triumphant state. These images stimulate the subconscious into accepting them as reality with the objective of directing certain behaviors accordingly. Visualizing also allows our imagination to increase and produce a stronger existence. There's truth to the saying 'use it or lose it.' It's a question of keeping your mind in shape to retain your mental abilities.

OBJECTIVE

Notes to Self are constant mental reminders of tasks to be completed as well as stored information in our subconscious minds. Speaking what's to be as if it was turns our thought into action and activates our nervous system.

Affirmations are usually short, but positive statements that help to defy and control self-sabotaging and negative thinking. When mental notes and affirmations are often repeated along with a genuine belief is when positive change takes place. For the record, anyone can repeat positive notes and affirmations when faced with situations and challenges. What elevates you is when you repeat these and others, feeling every word in your spirit. This takes you to another level.

NOTE TO SELF ONE
Let It All Go

NOTE TO SELF: It's not exactly simple and easy to release past issues and in many cases, it can be downright difficult while not knowing how it affects us. Harboring pain is never comfortable but accepting accountability and focusing on the future versus the past is the inception to healing. I will let go of the past to advance into my future since nothing can change it and I'll never accomplish my goals if I allow this to hinder my progress. If I continue in a reversed course, then I'll never advance forward and run great risks of becoming involved in mental and emotional ruin.

AFFIRM: I'm releasing what no longer serves me. I will also release everything that holds me back from progressing, including relationships, failures, fears, and insecurities because I'm over all of it.

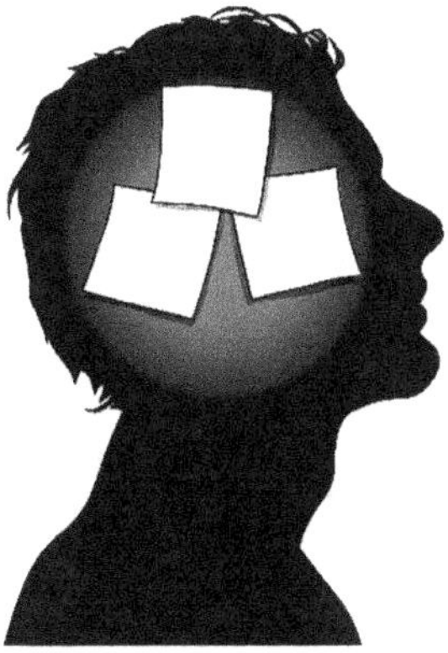

YOUR THOUGHTS OF YOU IN WORDS...

Your Thoughts Of You In Words...

NOTE TO SELF TWO
Change and Growth

NOTE TO SELF: Change is inevitable. When I choose to grow through life and not just go through life, is the point when I recognize the feelings of accomplishment, achievement, and completion. Each day, I have a chance and a choice knowing change is mandatory while growth is optional.

AFFIRM: My journey is never considered a race, so I will grant myself the space and time to learn and even more change and grow.

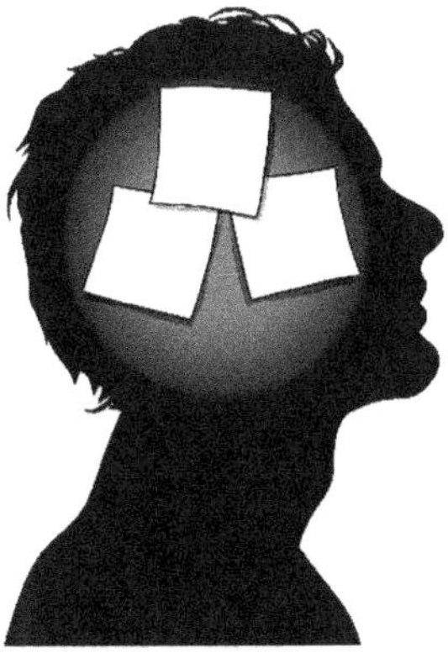

Your Thoughts Of You In Words...

YOUR THOUGHTS OF YOU IN WORDS...

Note To Self Three
Welcoming Challenges

NOTE TO SELF: Challenges are often new and can require great effort, determination, and often have limitless benefits. If I never welcome challenges, then I'll never embrace change. If I never embrace change, then I'll never receive growth, and this defeats my purpose. As a result, I'll never witness the beginning phase of my developmental structure increasing my knowledge and creating additional opportunities.

AFFIRM: By embracing and overcoming all challenges I will attract and receive abundance in my life.

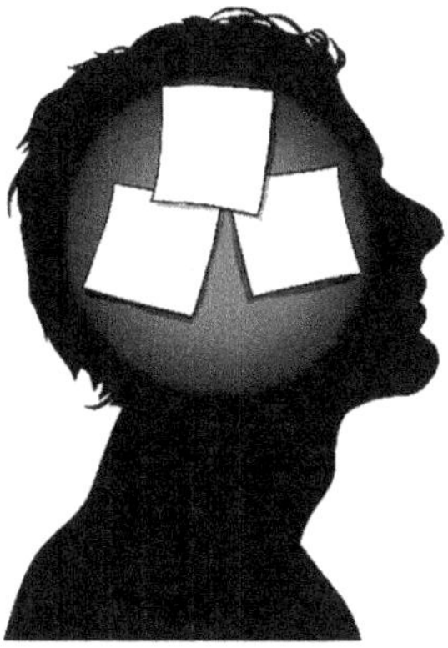

Your Thoughts Of You In Words...

Your Thoughts Of You In Words...

NOTE TO SELF FOUR
Raising Standards

NOTE TO SELF: Determining what I think of myself and breaking through limited beliefs will help to raise my standards and upgrade my life. Increasing my standards is never about being vain or self-centered. Raising my standards and lowering my tolerance is another way to assist me in reaching my destination to escape economic bondage.

AFFIRM: First, I will believe and have faith in myself that I can attain by becoming more assertive and using positive self-talk, I can raise my personal standard while lowering my tolerance of un-optimistic thoughts, views, and opinions. By overcoming the negative voice in my head and conquering my fear it will enhance my productivity, raising my quality of living.

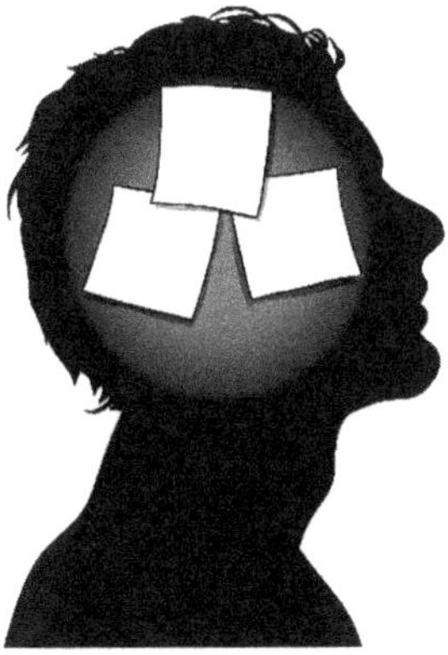

Your Thoughts Of You In Words...

YOUR THOUGHTS OF YOU IN WORDS...

NOTE TO SELF FIVE
Mind Over Matter

NOTE TO SELF: It takes only a minimum amount of determination and desire to understand the meaning of mind over matter. Mind over matter characterizes the achievement over physical interference. Unfortunately, life never presented any of us with an instructional video or a hard copy of standard operating procedures.

Therefore, I understand I can manage all situations and circumstances by the power of my thinking. What matters most is my mind, which is my way of thinking and from where all things are conceived.

AFFIRM: I'm always learning and growing, and I will always keep in mind what matters and what does not.

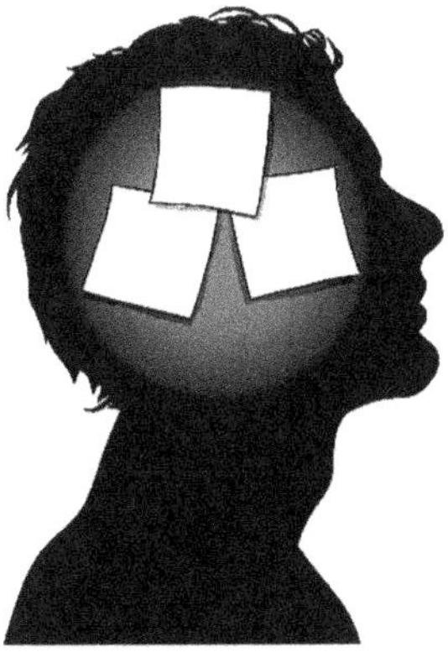

YOUR THOUGHTS OF YOU IN WORDS...

YOUR THOUGHTS OF YOU IN WORDS...

Note To Self Six
True Wealth

NOTE TO SELF: Like so many, I grew up thinking being wealthy meant having an abundance of money, a massive house, and a luxury vehicle. Unfortunately, most are still confused, believing money will solve all issues.

Our culture suggests success will be discovered at the next income bracket, but that only works in a perfect world. I can climb to the top of every ladder pursuing fame, power, and wealth and at the same time be completely unhappy, depressed, and unfulfilled. My perception of true wealth is when all life needs are met. This is discovered by performing a simple self-evaluation with the outcome of having all my needs met is where true wealth, fulfillment, and happiness lies.

AFFIRM: I will focus on shifting my life starting with my over perspective to accomplishing goals I look to achieve.

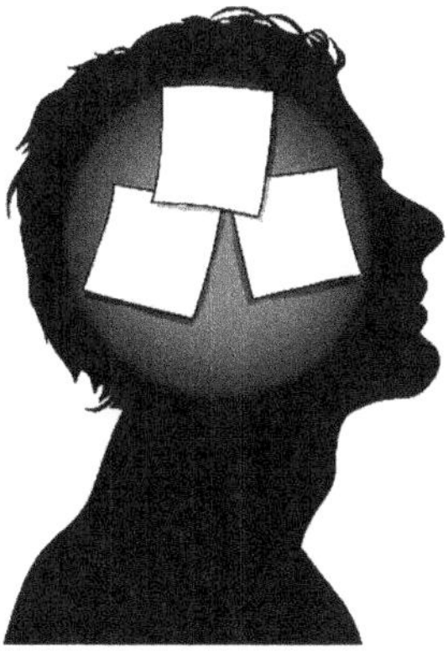

YOUR THOUGHTS OF YOU IN WORDS...

Your Thoughts Of You In Words...

Note To Self Seven
The Same Place

NOTE TO SELF: If I'm still in the same place I was five years ago, then I'm just going through life instead of growing through life and there is a difference. How can I benefit from doing the same things and expect different results? This is a form of insanity and defined as extreme foolishness.

AFFIRM: I will pledge to getting unstuck in life by making small changes including having faith in myself. I can reach expectations and get out of my comfort zone without sabotaging my progress. I will search for my passion and what makes me feel alive.

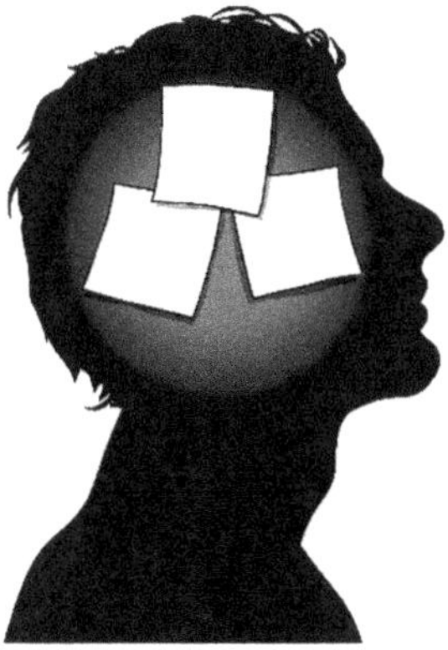

Your Thoughts Of You In Words...

Your Thoughts Of You In Words...

Note To Self Eight
Stepping Out of The Box

NOTE TO SELF: Of the many foundations for authentic supremacy in life arises my ability to make certain moves, especially during times of great difficulty and anxiety. When I think outside the box, I become a better version of myself, which is most significant. This is the inception phase of expanding all options and stepping into greatness.

AFFIRM: I will decrease then eliminate all limits on my own judgment and actions. This increases my likelihood of more positive outcomes and eventually expands the odds of ultimately reaching my intended target. It's critical to change my space, get away from typical routines to find creative ideas and solutions.

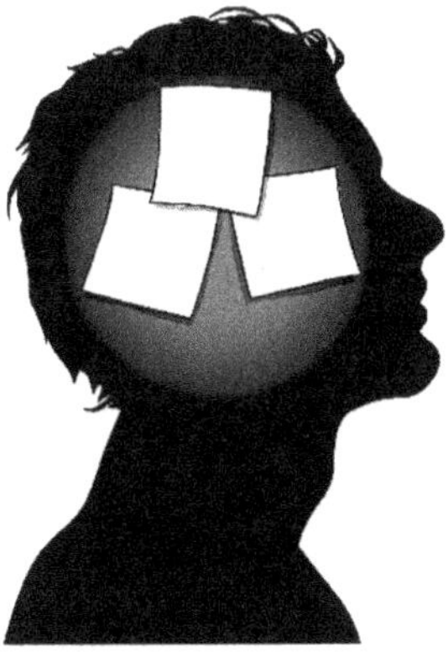

Your Thoughts Of You In Words...

YOUR THOUGHTS OF YOU IN WORDS...

Note To Self Nine
Attitude

NOTE TO SELF: Attitude is a psychological paradigm that directly involves my mindset, feelings, and overall viewpoint towards people and situations. By developing and maintaining a positive attitude, the benefits are never-ending. This includes a longer life span, and a stronger immune system resisting certain physical and mental illnesses. This can also lower the rate of depression, stress, and deliver a better psychological wellbeing. This defines and delimits my level of success and state of mind allowing me to vision and expect greater things to come.

AFFIRM: I can develop a winning and positive attitude by interacting in environments with people that reinforce me in a different way.

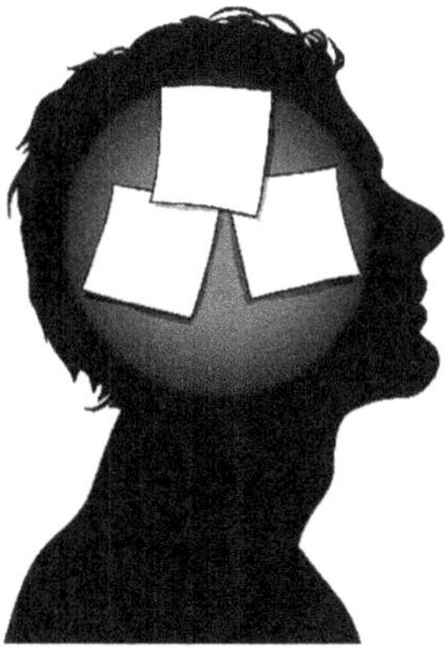

Your Thoughts Of You In Words...

YOUR THOUGHTS OF YOU IN WORDS...

NOTE TO SELF TEN
Comfort Zone

NOTE TO SELF: My comfort zone is a psychological and familiar state of mind in which I normally feel the safest. In my zone is where I'm most acquainted with low levels of anxiety and stress. This also relates to personal and professional relationships. I must embrace all fears and step out of my comfort zone and explore the unknown. I have missed countless opportunities due to fear, laziness, ignorance, and the love of instant gratification.

AFFIRM: There are no incentives to reach new heights of performance in my comfort zone. Starting with my daily routine I will develop new habits and take certain risks to reverse the plateau on my progress. I will commit to seeking temporary inconvenience in order to obtain the rewards of extended positive results.

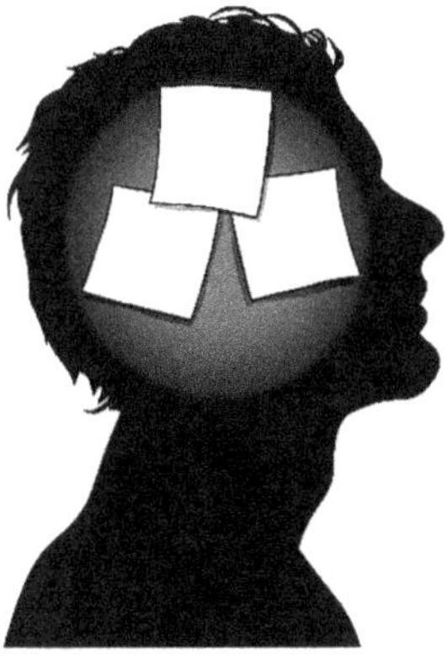

YOUR THOUGHTS OF YOU IN WORDS...

Your Thoughts Of You In Words...

NOTE TO SELF ELEVEN
Surrounded by Success

NOTE TO SELF: Proverbs teaches that "iron sharpens iron." Ancient writers realized the most common metal in the world could indeed sharpen other iron elements. In other terms, wise people should question, coach, encourage, and educate, building one another.

This simple statement assures me that I'm never alone on my journey and in order to make myself better there is a mutual benefit in making others better as well. When surrounded with others who are on similar paths it becomes less difficult to remain focused on my goals. If I surround myself with success, then eventually success will rub off on me. When choosing to associate myself with and the amount of time awarded, creates a major impact on my conclusion.

AFFIRM: It's often said in order to change what I know I need to change who I know. I will continuously commit to emulating the success of others.

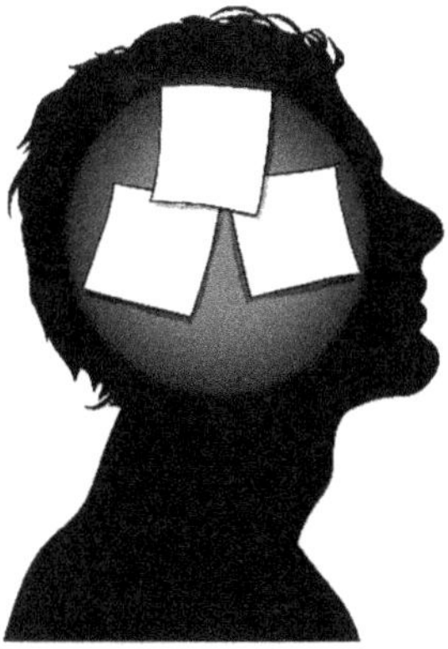

Your Thoughts Of You In Words...

Your Thoughts Of You In Words...

Note To Self Twelve
Communicating

NOTE TO SELF: Communication skills are an integral part of life. It is a two-way process involving the transferring of information and messages from one person to another. The word communication is derived from the Latin word communicare, meaning to share, participate or transmit. Effective communication skills are fundamental to succeed in all areas of life. When you are obligated to enhance this verbally and nonverbally it builds better character and relationships.

AFFIRM: I plan to witness my network of beneficial professional relationships increase and as a result create endless opportunities beyond all expectations.

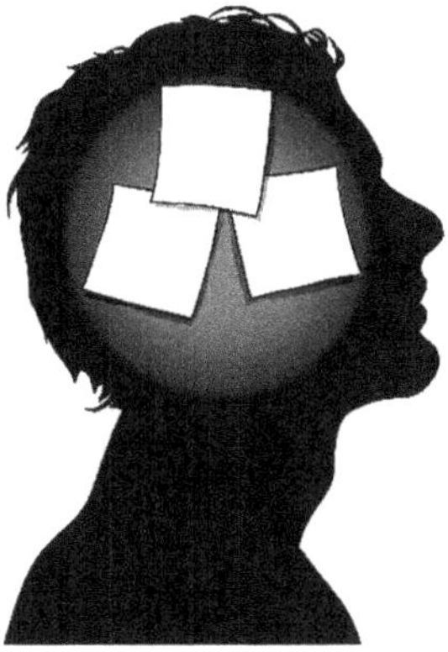

Your Thoughts Of You In Words...

Your Thoughts Of You In Words...

NOTE TO SELF THIRTEEN
Assets and Liabilities

NOTE TO SELF: In my personal journey of becoming a more effective and influential business professional, I had to learn who were assets and who were liabilities. Some may have good intentions while others might have ulterior motives. Therefore, even indirect relationships could still be bad for business.

Several people are assets, which add significant value while others can be considered liabilities, which are transactions causing my net worth to depreciate.

AFFIRM: I will learn the variation of those that place me in the green and those that position me in the red for future reference.

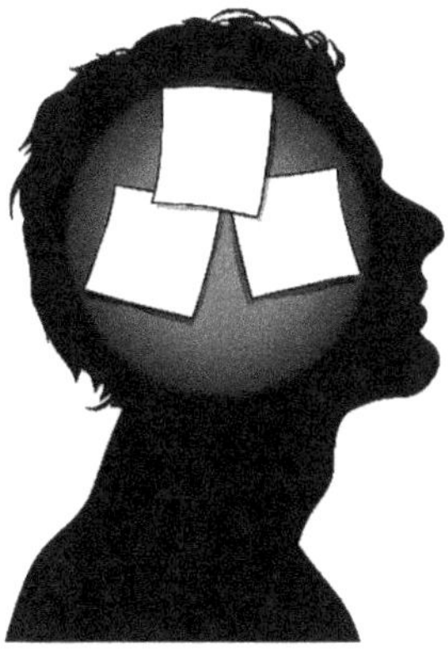

Your Thoughts Of You In Words...

YOUR THOUGHTS OF YOU IN WORDS...

Note To Self Fourteen
Control

NOTE TO SELF: To become even more fruitful, I must take stock of the portions of my life where I contain complete control. Understanding what I can control eliminates valuable time and energy worrying and putting forth much needed effort on things that are out of reach. In short, it benefits me greatly to convert emphasis, time, and energy where it will be most beneficial in my efforts to reach more goals. I have control over my character, health, education, level of productivity, and financial security.

AFFIRM: I will not submit or surrender these areas to determine my outcome under any circumstance. I refuse to exist in servitude to the past, fears, the economy, past failures and others.

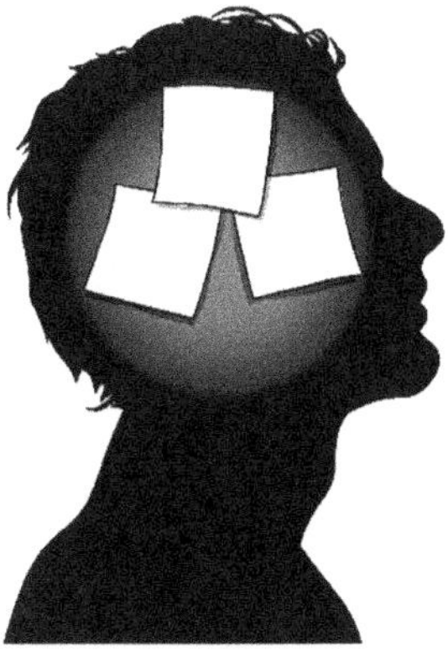

Your Thoughts Of You In Words...

Your Thoughts Of You In Words...

NOTE TO SELF FIFTEEN
It's Necessary

NOTE TO SELF: Because I don't consider myself to be a perfect person, it's necessary that I complete a self-evaluation understanding all needed areas of improvement. It's also necessary that I never reveal my plans to anyone but show my results instead. It's necessary that I never settle because life is worth much more and its compensation will be much greater only when I remember what's necessary.

AFFIRM: I will repeat that It was necessary to go through what I did yesterday to get to where I am today. The same applies for tomorrow as I take life day by day because it's necessary.

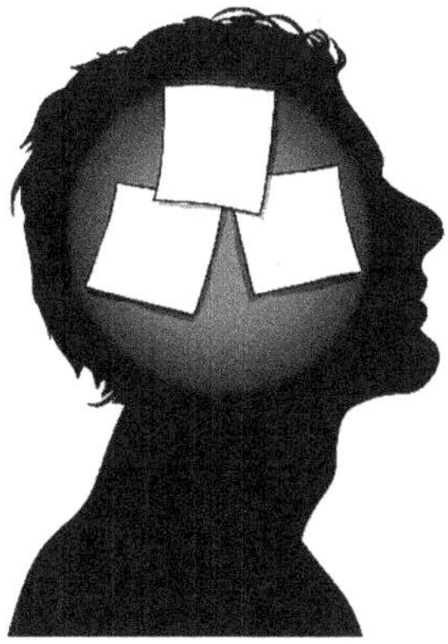

Your Thoughts Of You In Words...

YOUR THOUGHTS OF YOU IN WORDS...

NOTE TO SELF SIXTEEN
Production & Consumption

NOTE TO SELF: Production is the process involving the creation of products or services over time. This method is carried out to satisfy human wants and needs. Examples of production are creating a business to serve the needs of others or patenting a product to fill a void or solve a need that others might have. Mentally speaking, acquiring a wealth of knowledge can also be considered production in a manner of speaking.

AFFIRM: In order to accomplish my goal, I will increase production and decrease consumption. Adopting this mindset allows room for the expansion of the process of improvement personally and professionally.

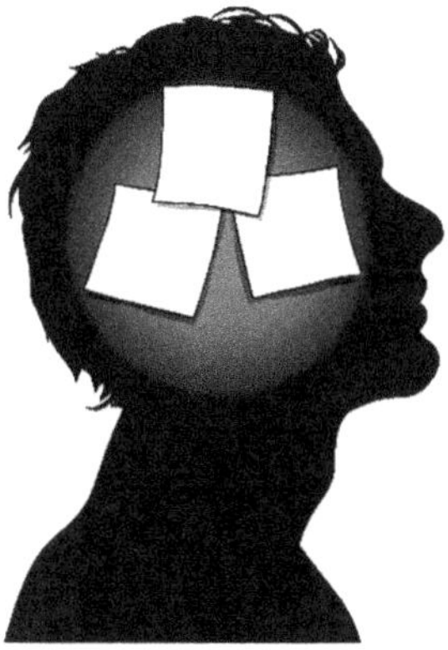

Your Thoughts Of You In Words...

YOUR THOUGHTS OF YOU IN WORDS...

Note To Self Seventeen
Priorities

NOTE TO SELF: Even though we recognize prioritizing is imperative to everyday life I was like some who allowed priorities to slip to the bottom of my daily list. What should we do? Without identifying clear priorities, it's tough to manage our time and achieve goals. What does it benefit me to allow my life to be consumed by things that are not priority?

AFFIRM: Creating a sense of direction often leads to greater accomplishments, better relationships and feeling of accomplishment. I will develop and stick to a routine to help prioritize daily tasks and goals. I will no longer give time and energy to people or things when I need it as well.

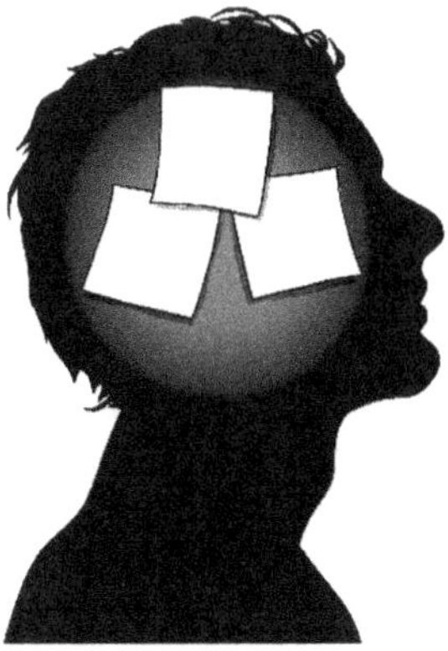

YOUR THOUGHTS OF YOU IN WORDS...

Your Thoughts Of You In Words...

Note To Self Eighteen
Self-Contained

NOTE TO SELF: Self-contained meaning to keep thoughts and private feelings private not dealing with help from others. Having a closed mind and self-containment gets me nowhere. History teaches this, but at times I refuse to embrace and accept the knowledge due to ignorance, which is the refusal of knowledge. With an unrestricted mindset, I can comprehend that life is much bigger and greater than me and those who surround me.

AFFIRM: Opening my mind unlocks potential, creates possibilities, and enlarges my network creating more opportunity. Closed minds don't expand and where there's no expansion there's very little development.

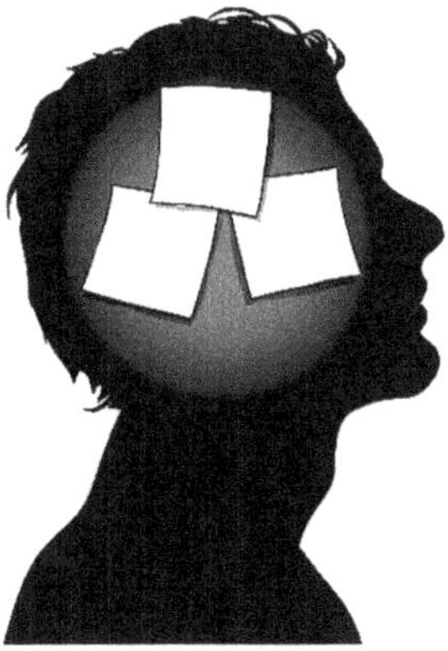

Your Thoughts Of You In Words...

Your Thoughts Of You In Words...

NOTE TO SELF NINETEEN
A Gift

NOTE TO SELF: My entire existence along with my mind are two of the greatest gifts. My mind is the creation of all personal perceptions as well as the focal point of my feelings and memories. At times, it can also be compared to muscles of the body. The more I exercise it, the greater my perception becomes. Outside of any tangible item I possess, my mind is my most prized possession, so I must be protected at all costs.

AFFIRM: By not restricting my mind and respecting the beliefs, practices and cultures of others I can build lasting relationships with whoever I meet. My mind can also be a powerful and priceless gift to the world, but a gift is useless when left in the box.

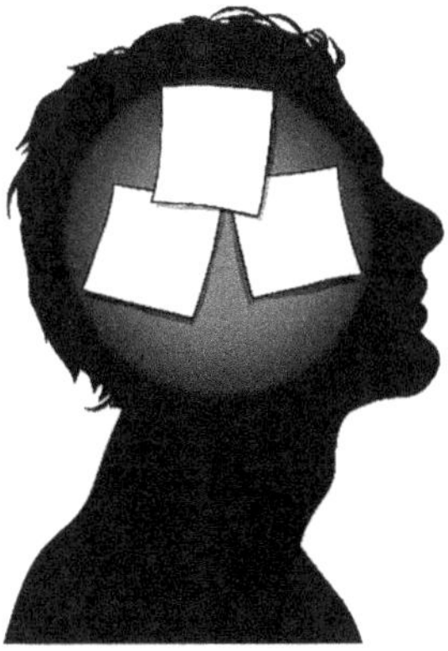

Your Thoughts Of You In Words...

Your Thoughts Of You In Words...

Note To Self Twenty
Setting Standards

NOTE TO SELF: Setting personal standards are paramount and are what separates achievers from everyone else. When setting high standards for myself, they allow me to guarantee a certain level of productivity. This ensures the quality where I expect to treat and be treated with the highest regards. Having low standards usually means things will be accepted as they are given with no question or negotiation.

AFFIRM: It's not a bad idea to set high standards, however, I cannot become obsessed with them. I will not strive for perfection but make attempts to gain progress in its place because progress is a step towards perfection.

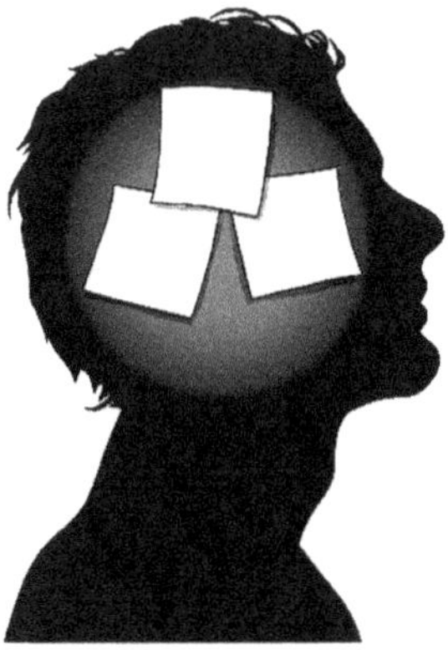

Your Thoughts Of You In Words...

Your Thoughts Of You In Words...

Note To Self Twenty-One
My Purpose

NOTE TO SELF:
"The two most important days in your life are the day you were born and the day you discovered why you were born."
                                                            -Mark Twain

In other words, it means discovering your purpose. My life's purpose consists of the motivating factors for getting up every morning. This guides all life decisions, influences, my performance and goals while creating meaningful and guided direction. The naked eye will never encounter this kind of vision as it was predestined to be viewed after discovering the concealed wealth of the subconscious mind.

AFFIRM: Discovering my passion is only the beginning. The moment I overcome self-sabotage and utilize self-discipline, is when I decrease any attempts of self-doubt allowing me to move onward at a record pace.

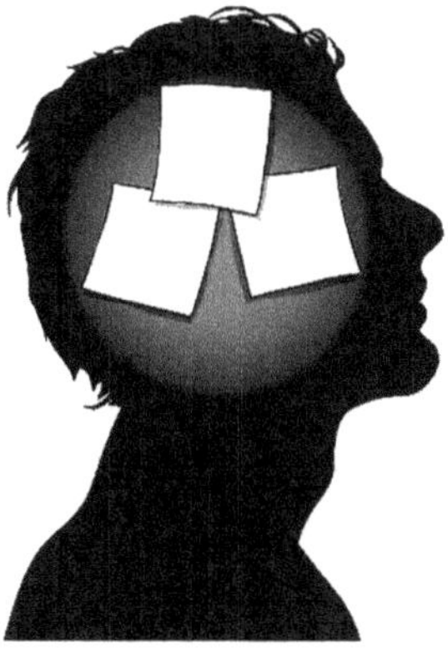

Your Thoughts Of You In Words...

Your Thoughts Of You In Words...

Note To Self Twenty-Two
Liberation

NOTE TO SELF: Liberation can be the act of setting yourself free from insecurities and emotional imprisonment. As I consciously liberate myself in efforts of living on purpose, I will continue to enlarge my territory by raising my standards and lowering my tolerance. I was not positioned at this point of existence to scrape the bottom so by adopting this new and innovative mindset it assigns me where I rightfully belong, which is at the top.

> "And as we let our own light shine, we unconsciously give other people permission to do the same. As we are liberated from our own fear, our presence automatically liberates others."
>
> Marianne Williamson

AFFIRM: Moving away from the expectations and demands of others is the beginning of living on my own terms. I start by respecting my intuition then questioning and breaking old patterns that no longer benefit my journey.

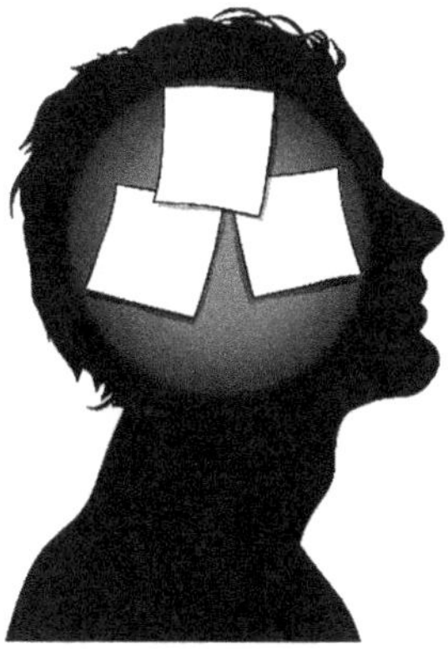

Your Thoughts Of You In Words...

Your Thoughts Of You In Words...

NOTE TO SELF TWENTY-THREE
Success

NOTE TO SELF: Success is a state or condition of meeting a defined range of expectations for myself. Success is not directly related to money. It's about self-fulfillment with a sense of achievement and accomplishment. When seeking my purpose and liberating myself from the financial aspect I will remember money is not the goal, it's an incentive.

AFFIRM: I will focus on doing more of what I love than waiting for doors to open for me. Passion is an instance or experience of strong desire following my heart. In pursuing it is the only way I'll discover total life fulfillment. I will focus on my passion because what I focus on more will grow expanding my potential.

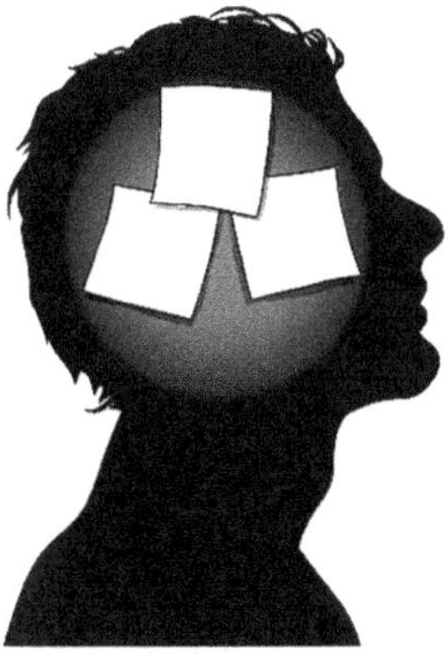

Your Thoughts Of You In Words...

Your Thoughts Of You In Words...

Note To Self Twenty-Four
Perceptions

NOTE TO SELF: Perception means the faculty of perceiving or apprehending by the means of the senses of the mind as we all live in different realities. It's necessary that after being labeled "at-risk" I remember to never allow the limited perceptions of others to define me or my reality. Although perceptions can influence, they also help understand the world around me. I will remember the thoughts of others are not my main concern and I must never confine myself with them as it greatly impacts my general emotional state.

AFFIRM: I will continuously utilize the process of my senses to become more aware of the environment around me because this supports me in so many ways.

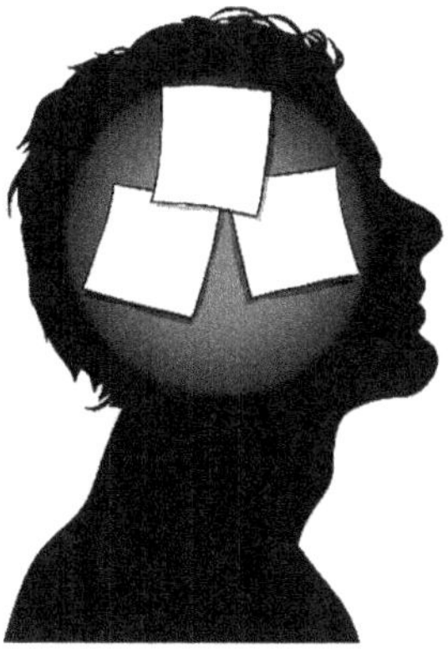

Your Thoughts Of You In Words...

Your Thoughts Of You In Words...

Note To Self Twenty-Five
Fell and Fail

NOTE TO SELF: While researching, I often reminisce about the late U. S. Representative Elijah Cummings' thought provoking commencement speech at Strayer University. He stated, "Don't mistake your commas for a period." I was at the edge of my seat as this charismatic elected official from the hood, (as he stated), delivered countless examples, which caused a continuous thunderous applause to pack the Baltimore, MD arena.

I recognize that a period indicates the end, however a comma symbolizes there is more to come. My loss of employment was a comma, so I kept writing about my life, my poor decision making was a comma, so I kept writing about my life. Each devastating experience was a comma also as this list can go on and on.

I remind myself and instruct others that falling is not failure. There is a difference between fell and fail. In the early years of my life, I fell several times. During my adolescent years, I fell quite often and as a young adult I fell over and over. Consequently, I refuse to ever fail because failure is not an option.

AFFIRM: Falling is failure only when I don't get up.

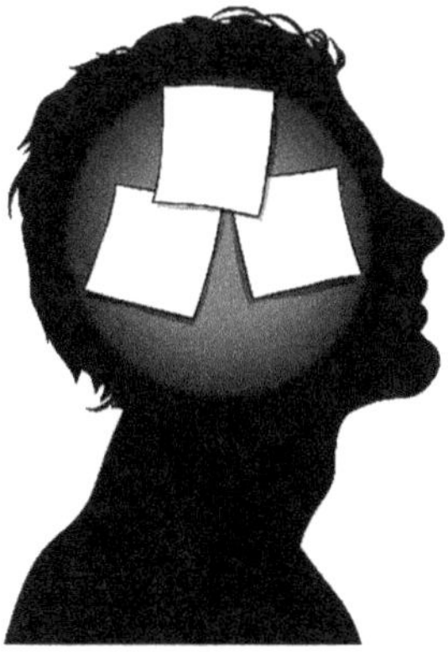

Your Thoughts Of You In Words...

Your Thoughts Of You In Words...

Note To Self Twenty-Six
Pain

NOTE TO SELF: Mental pain can be meaningfully applied to the study of different mental states, life conditions, and transitions. The fact that we were born does not mean we have arrived. Because it can take years to understand why we were sent here, our purpose in life can sometimes be found during a painful period. I choose to remain conscious to the thought that I will not perish from experiencing some mental pain, discomfort or distress throughout my transition. Quitting is not an option at this point of my life and won't take away any discomfort of growth.

AFFIRM: I'm repeating to myself that since I'm already in pain I might as well reap the benefits of it. Throwing in the towel is not an option and I should complete the task set before me in order to obtain a reward from it. At the end of all the problems and enduring some pain, there is a solution.

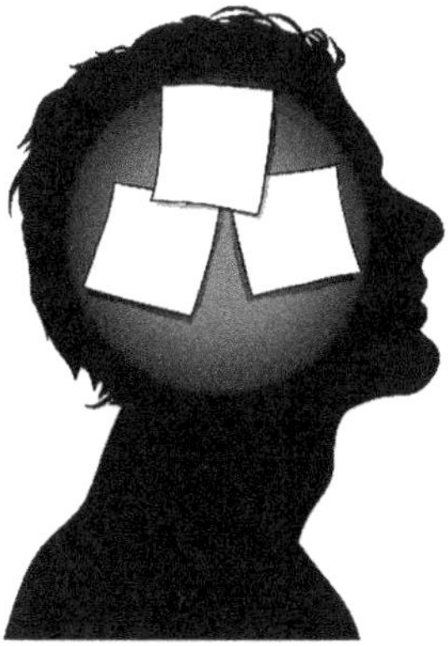

Your Thoughts Of You In Words...

Your Thoughts Of You In Words...

Note To Self Twenty-Seven
The Picture

NOTE TO SELF: In a perfect world, everyone would have no mistakes, issues, or shortcomings. I step out of the frame to see my picture and according to what I see, complete a full self-analysis. This is the inception of inner standing me.

AFFIRM: During this self-assessment, I will remain transparent while identifying my goals, accomplishments, strengths and weaknesses based on certain factors. By completing this it helps me to build confidence in my abilities, become more aware, accountable, and enhance certain skills.

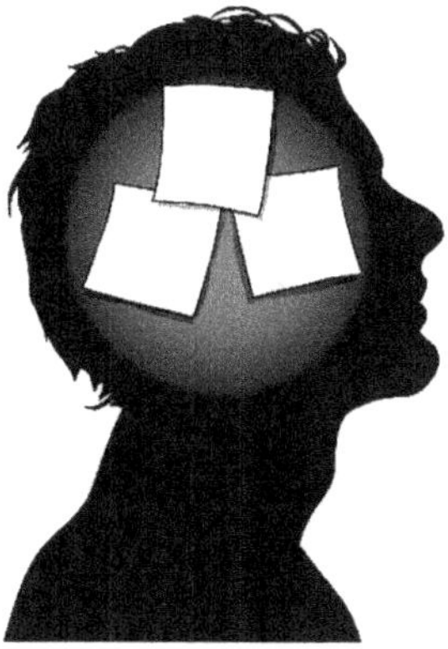

Your Thoughts Of You In Words...

Your Thoughts Of You In Words...

Note To Self Twenty-Eight
Completion

NOTE TO SELF: Completion is not optional, it's mandatory. Completion grants clarity and keeps our imagination from becoming stagnated. I will instruct and constantly remind myself that if there are no strategies of finishing, then starting is no more than a waste of time for myself and others.

AFFIRM: I need to bring complete closure to many incomplete things in my life in order to clear the path for my envisioned future. I will not start something I can't finish, nor will I allow something to get started that I can't conclude. I will complete the task, accomplish the goal or among other terms, succeed, or die trying.

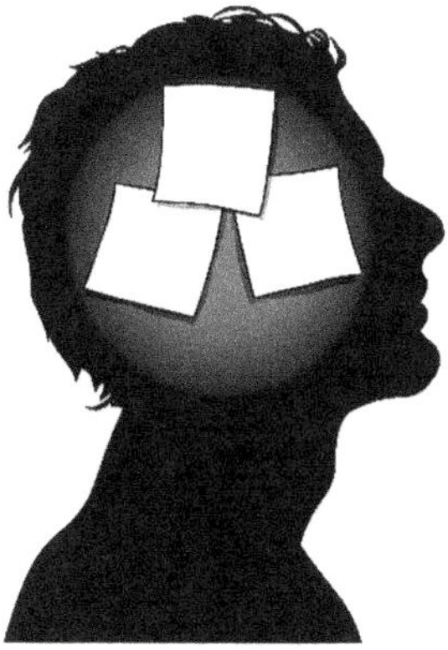

Your Thoughts Of You In Words...

Your Thoughts Of You In Words...

NOTE TO SELF TWENTY-NINE
Competing

NOTE TO SELF: Competition is a rivalry where two or more parties or groups strive for a common unshareable goal. I constantly think about winning so there's a good chance I worry about losing; however, life is not a competition. It profits me in no way to try and compete against others. Even with an extremely competitive mentality, I will no longer concern myself with the efforts of others and center my attention on my own development and purpose.

AFFIRM: Comparing my journey to others is common, but it's important to train myself to cease because constant comparison can ultimately lead to negative thoughts. If you'll notice certain comparison triggers and make plans to avoid them at all costs. I recognize competing can become a harmful pattern and no two minds think alike as things will be interpreted differently. This new approach releases much needed time to compete against myself to advance to my next ranking.

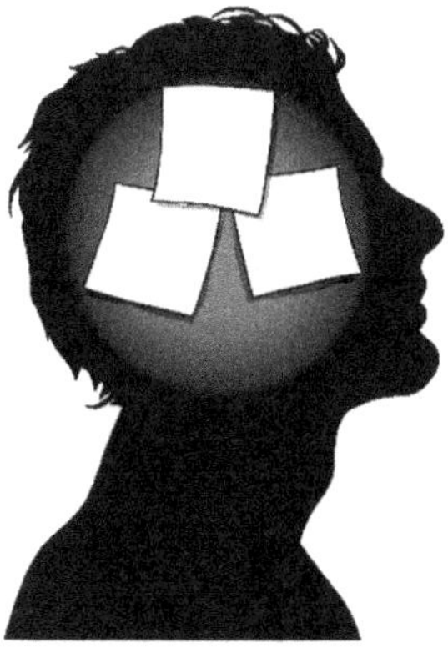

YOUR THOUGHTS OF YOU IN WORDS...

Your Thoughts Of You In Words...

Note To Self Thirty
Accountability

NOTE TO SELF: The willingness to accept full responsibility for my own actions is when accountability is conceived. When we hold ourselves personally liable and accountable, we take complete ownership of what happens as a result of our choices and actions. We don't blame others or make excuses, and you do what you can to make amends when things go wrong.

AFFIRM: Poor accountability is the result of underlying issues such as unclear vision and responsibilities. To become more accountable, I will remain transparent while confirming I'm clear about my roles and obligations. When I'm honest with myself and my role, then I can admit this and focus on the process of improvement. This helps to manage and make the most of my time.

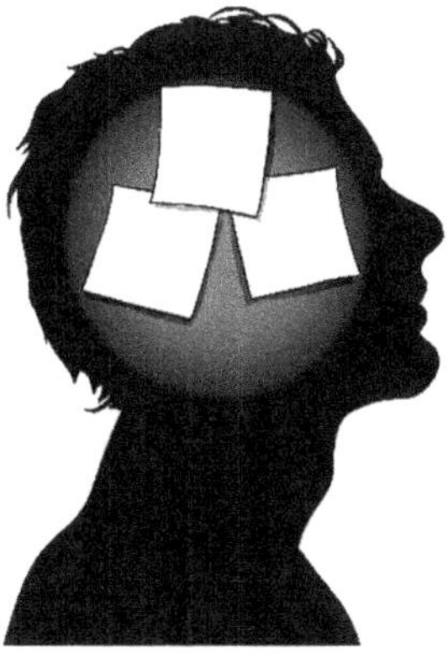

Your Thoughts Of You In Words...

YOUR THOUGHTS OF YOU IN WORDS...

"It's important what thoughts you are feeding into your mind because your thoughts create your belief and experiences. You have positive thoughts, and you have negative ones too. Nurture your mind with positive thoughts: kindness, empathy, compassion, peace, love, joy, humility, generosity, etc. The more you feed your mind with positive thoughts, the more you can attract great things into your life."

-Roy T. Bennett

Meet the Author

Brian P. is a native Carolinian who makes moves empowering individuals and groups in the community. He is a recognized sales professional where he utilizes his skills and talents to build relationships. He's also an empowerment speaker where he gives inspirational and informative talks to large and small groups. Past topics are: Overcoming obstacles, Embracing Change, Self-Development, and Personal Growth.

Additionally, he's an entrepreneur, he has served on the Mecklenburg County Juvenile Crime Prevention Council and was recognized in Who's Who in Black Charlotte.

Brian calls North Carolina home and reminds audiences we only pass through here once time and to get all you can out of life because life will get all it can out of you. He mostly enjoys grilling, hiking, exercising, and creating memories vacationing with his family whenever possible.

BOOK BRIAN

Website: www.mynotestoself.co

E-mail: info@mynotestoself.co

Facebook: Brian Peay

IG: @Bpspeaks

(800) 249-4509 Ext. 801

Go to www.mynotestoself.co
to sign up and receive news and information.

www.ingramcontent.com/pod-product-compliance
Lightning Source LLC
Chambersburg PA
CBHW071350080526
44587CB00017B/3041